ADVENTURE TIME™

Who in the Land of Ooo Are You?

by Brandon

PS
Price Ste
An Imprint of Pengu... LLC

PRICE STERN SLOAN
Published by the Penguin Group
Penguin Group (USA) LLC, 375 Hudson Street, New York, New York 10014, USA

USA ι Canada ι UK ι Ireland ι Australia ι New Zealand ι India ι South Africa ι China

penguin.com
A Penguin Random House Company

Published in 2015 by Price Stern Sloan, a division of Penguin Young Readers Group, 345 Hudson Street, New York, New York 10014. PSS! is a registered trademark of Penguin Group (USA) LLC. Printed in the USA.

ISBN 978-0-8431-8076-3   10 9 8 7 6 5 4 3 2 1

WELCOME TO THE LAND OF OOO!

You're going to meet so many awesome people and go on a ton of cool adventures. It's a great time to be YOU. But the question on everyone's mind is— ARE YOU READY? There's a lot of stuff to see and do in the Land of Ooo, and you'll need to be prepared for anything. The first step is getting to know yourself. This book is filled with pop quizzes and other creative stuff that will help you learn more about who you are and what you like. Knowing about yourself is super important, so get that brain in gear and use your imagination. Someday when you're an old person, you'll be able to look back at your answers and think, "Hey! I was a cool kid once!"

CONTENTS

WHO ARE YOU?

First things first! Before you go on your journey through the Land of Ooo, make sure you answer these questions so you know a little bit more about yourself. And if you don't have an answer for something, just make it up!

What's your name?

....

What's your name in the Land of Ooo?

....

How old are you?

....

What's the date today?

....

What's your best pal's name?

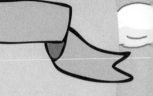

....

If you could go anywhere in the universe, where would you go?

....

....

....

What is your secret superpower?

....

....

....

What instrument do you play?

....

....

....

WHATCHA INTO?

It's time to find out a few more things about what kind of stuff you like to see and do. You can never know enough about yourself.

So . . . whatcha into?

What are your top three favorite books?

1. ....
2. ....
3. ....

What are your top three favorite TV shows?

1. ....
2. ....
3. ....

What are your top three favorite movies?

1. ....
2. ....
3. ....

Who are your top three favorite monsters?

1. ....
2. ....
3. ....

What are your top three favorite kinds of candy?

1. ....

2. ....

3. ....

What's your favorite game?

....

What's your favorite food to throw at people?

....

What's your favorite subject in school?

....

What's your favorite place to vacation?

....

What's your favorite animal?

....

Circle your answer:

PANTS **OR** NO PANTS

PENCIL **OR** PEN   BREAKFAST **OR** DINNER

RED **OR** BLUE

ROCK AND ROLL **OR** POP MUSIC

VIDEO GAME **OR** BOARD GAME

MORNING **OR** NIGHT

CITY **OR** COUNTRY

BASEBALL **OR** FOOTBALL

DOLL **OR** ACTION FIGURE

THE STORY OF
YOUR LIFE

YOU are the only you in the entire world. Isn't that crazy? And only YOU can tell the world the story of your life. Start at the beginning with your earliest memory. Then tell us about where you came from and how things have been going for you so far. Oh, and don't forget to mention your friends and family. They're really important. Here's your big chance. Don't screw this up. On your mark, get set . . . GO!

BRO TIME!

A bro is pretty much your best friend in the whole wide world. And a bro can be a boy OR a girl. That's pretty freaky, but it's pretty cool, too. How much do you know about your bro? Take this quiz and find out.

Who is your #1 bro?

....

What's your favorite quality about your #1 bro?

....

If your #1 bro were a magical dog, what would his/her name be?

....

If you had to describe your #1 bro in one word, what would it be?

....

If you and your #1 bro were in a video game, what would it be called?

....

Which of these things do you like to do with your bro?

toot contest   mud wrestling   tickle torture   movie night

Which of these desserts would you make for your bro's birthday?

boysenberry pie   dump cake   broccoli brownies   puddin'

How do you greet your bro?

with a firm handshake   "What up, bro?"   a high five   with a bro hug

Has your bro ever seen you cry?   YES or NO

Would you let your bro wear sweatpants outside?   YES or NO

Does your bro know a secret about you?   YES or NO

Would you help your bro bite a giant's butt?   YES or NO

Have you ever tricked your bro into thinking he or she is a robot?   YES or NO

ACTION CARDS!

You've completed the first section. Congratulations! You deserve your own Action Card. It's what all young adventurers have, just like Finn and Jake. You're going to be the coolest person around, like, really soon. Fill in the details on the opposite page, and be careful when you cut along the dotted lines. We know you're not a baby, but maybe safety scissors, okay?

HELPFUL HINTS

1 An ALIAS is like a nickname.

2 Paste your favorite photo of yourself on your Action Card.

3 Give someone the WILD CARD and watch them go **CRAZY!**

WILD CARD!!!
GO CRAZY!!!
YEAH!!!
THIS CARD IS WILD!!!
WILD LIKE A RIVER!!!

NAME: Jake the Dog
ALIAS: Randy Butternubs

NAME: Finn the Human
ALIAS: Prince Hotbod

WILD CARD!!!
GO CRAZY!!!
THIS CARD IS WILD!!!
YEAH!!!

NAME:
ALIAS:

FINN & JAKE: THE BUDDY SYSTEM

Now that we know who YOU are a little bit, it's time to meet your guides through the Land of Ooo—Finn and Jake! They just happen to be super-awesome best friends who do everything together. You'll probably become their third super best friend by the end of this book. Maybe they'll invite you to live with them in the Tree Fort?!

A bro can dream . . .

PARTY IN THE TREE FORT

Finn and Jake's Tree Fort is where all the action is goin' down. Woo-hoo! Party time all the time! Okay maybe not ALL the time, but those guys do like to party. What kinds of parties do YOU like?

What are three cool party themes?

1. .... 2. .... 3. ....

What are your top three party snacks?

1. .... 2. .... 3. ....

Who would you invite to a party?

....

....

....

What three movies would you watch at a party?

1. .... 2. .... 3. ....

What are your favorite party games?

....

....

What kind of decorations do you put up when you
have a party?

....

....

AWKWARD QUESTIONS

Sometimes when Finn and Jake are alone together, they'll ask each other awkward questions. It can get pretty weird. The next time you're alone with your friends, ask them some of the questions below. Write down their answers, too, so there's a record of their weirdness.

Do you believe in magic? **YES** or **NO**

Have you ever been stung by a jellyfish? **YES** or **NO**

Would you eat a live worm if you were bored? **YES** or **NO**

Do you like hot cheese? **YES** or **NO**

Would you ever walk around in a feather cape? **YES** or **NO**

If you were a talking animal, what animal would you be, and what would you say? **YES** or **NO**

....

....

What would you do if your head turned into a pumpkin?

....

....

If you could read anyone's mind in the whole entire world, who would it be, and why?

....

....

What's your favorite flavor of cough medicine? Why?

....

....

What would you name the perfect hug?

Super Squeezy   Noodle Arms   Grandfather's Armpit   TOO TIGHT

If scientists discovered a new season, what would it be called?

Chillin' Time   Just Right   The Windy Interval   Red-hot Pizza Summer

If you were a crazed supervillain, what would your name be?

Lake Guy   The Tinkler

Lady Hair-ington   Chirp

What would your boat be called?

Shore Thang   Life's a Beach

Francesca   Boat

BUCKET LIST

Finn's pal Billy was the most awesome warrior you've ever seen. Seriously, he was THE BEST. Billy was a big dreamer, too, so he made a bucket list of all the things he wanted to do in his life before he kicked the bucket (died). Then he was destroyed by the Lich. Don't be too sad, because now Billy's spirit has ascended to the 50th Dead World, where he's spending his afterlife doing all kinds of Billy stuff.

WE MISS YOU, BILLY!!!!

So . . . what's on YOUR bucket list?

DISGUISE-O-RAMA

Jake is a master of disguise, and don't you forget it. The cool part of being a master of disguise is making up a backstory for your character that's totally different from your own. Make up some backstory and stuff about Jake's different characters.

What's your secret spy code name?

How would you disguise yourself?

What's your favorite kind of mustache?

NAME:
....

SECRET MISSION:
....

BACKSTORY:
....

....

....

....

NAME:
....

SECRET MISSION:
....

BACKSTORY:
....

....

....

....

NAME:
....

SECRET MISSION:
....

BACKSTORY:
....

....

....

....

JAKE THE DOG
THE QUIZ

You think you know Jake the Dog, but you have NO IDEA! Take this quiz and find out.

1. Jake once shape-shifted into the form of a female Cinnamon Bun.

TRUE or FALSE

2. Jake knows how to make Korean food.

TRUE or FALSE

3. Jake has a secret diary that he calls "The Puppington Chronicles."

TRUE or FALSE

4. Jake has a brother named Jermaine.

TRUE or FALSE

5. Jake and Finn became brothers when they shared an ice-cream cone together.

TRUE or FALSE

6. Jake loves chocolate because he's a dog.

TRUE or FALSE

7. Jake knows how to read Braille.

TRUE or FALSE

8. Jake solves mysteries as Professor K'Nine.

TRUE or FALSE

9. Jake loves to dance.

TRUE or FALSE

10. Jake once thought that he was the Gut Grinder.

TRUE or FALSE

What is the name of Jake's newspaper column?

A. Jake's World

B. Stretching the Truth with Jake the Dog

C. Begs the Question

D. Me & My Dawgs

Jake has what kind of power?

A. The Power of Persuasion

B. Stinky Butt Power

C. Stretchy Power

D. The Power of Love

Which of these people has Jake farted on?

A. The Fruit Witches

B. The Apple Bottoms

C. The Candy Vampires

D. Who HASN'T Jake farted on, am I right?

Jake is very good at playing which of these board games?

A. Card Wars

B. Toilet Assault

C. War Cards

D. Hungry Hungry Grandma

Who is Jake's girlfriend?

A. Finn

B. Lady Rainicorn

C. Marceline

D. His work!

Jake's body is filled with which of these things?

A. The dark power of the Cupcake Lord

B. Carp

C. Little baby nachos

D. The energy of a thousand partying demons

FINN THE HUMAN
THE QUIZ

You think you know Finn the Human, but you have NO IDEA! Take this quiz and find out.

1. Princess Bubblegum once used Finn's DNA to create a candy sphinx. **TRUE or FALSE**

2. Finn always wears red footie pajamas to bed. **TRUE or FALSE**

3. Finn is Duke of the Goblins. **TRUE or FALSE**

4. Finn was once turned into a Hug Wolf. **TRUE or FALSE**

5. Sometimes Finn goes boom-boom. **TRUE or FALSE**

6. Finn has never ever taken his hat off in his entire life. **TRUE or FALSE**

7. Finn was once turned into a cat by the Grand Master Wizard. **TRUE or FALSE**

8. Finn is deathly afraid of dancing. **TRUE or FALSE**

9. The only person who can tickle Finn is the Ice King. **TRUE or FALSE**

10. Billy is one of Finn's heroes. **TRUE or FALSE**

What is Finn's favorite food?

A. Cheese nuggets

B. Stew

C. Saucy sauce with cheeseburgers on top

D. Meat loaf

Finn once wore a mustache disguise and called himself which of these names?

A. Francis Murtaugh

B. Davey

C. Shoko

D. Mister Sellecktar

How old is Finn?

A. Age ain't nothing but a number, son

B. A zillion years young

C. As old as he wants to be!

D. NONE OF THE ABOVE

Finn was once trapped in which of these places?

A. The cupboard

B. A realm full of pillows

C. A prison within his own mind

D. Behind a haunted desk

When Finn is all dressed up in a fancy tuxedo, he goes by which of these names?

A. Prince Hotbod

B. Finntastic

C. Admiral Fancy T. Pants

D. Tux Lonestar

Finn once helped the Box Prince reclaim his throne. What does the Box Prince look like?

A. A box with a prince on its head

B. A cat with a box on its head

C. A head with a prince on its cat

D. A prince with a cat in a box

BMO in the House

HELLO! WELCOME TO THE BMO PARTY. LET'S BOOGIE.

Yeah, yeah, yeah! It's a super crazy time! BMO's here to rock the party right! Did you know BMO can do just about anything? Not only is it one of Finn and Jake's best pals, it can also play video games, sing songs, be a toaster or dance like a funky machine. Answer these questions so BMO knows a little more about YOU.

What are your three best qualities?

1. _____ 2. _____ 3. _____

What are three things you like to do when you're alone?

1. _____ 2. _____ 3. _____

What one thing do you wish you could do better?

_____

_____

What is one thing you'd like to try?

What scares you? -------------------------------

Do you like to...?

Write songs	**YES** or **NO**
Make up stories	**YES** or **NO**
Eat sandwiches	**YES** or **NO**
Tap-dance	**YES** or **NO**
Climb trees	**YES** or **NO**
Boil eggs	**YES** or **NO**
Braid hair	**YES** or **NO**
Smile	**YES** or **NO**
Laugh	**YES** or **NO**
Eat broccoli soup	**YES** or **NO**
Talk to dolls	**YES** or **NO**
Read books	**YES** or **NO**
Ride a bike	**YES** or **NO**
Wear dresses	**YES** or **NO**
Play dodgeball	**YES** or **NO**

Pretend Time

Here's a little secret: When no one is around, BMO likes to pretend. Sometimes it pretends to be a smart detective looking for mysteries, and other times it pretends to be a fun-loving kid. Pretend time is the best. YOU should pretend that you're someone else. Fill out the answers below to create your own pretend character. Make up anything you want.

It's PRETEND TIME!

What is your pretend character's name?

Where does your pretend character live?

What is your pretend character's job?

How old is your pretend character?

What does your pretend character wear?

What is your pretend character's favorite dinner?

Tell a story about the first time your pretend character went to the circus:

Tell a story about the time your pretend character went to a family reunion:

Tell a story about your pretend character's favorite birthday:

A Day in the Life

BMO leads a very exciting life, and it can be hard to remember all the cool stuff it does. That's why it keeps a journal. Now it's your turn to keep a record of the day's events. First, choose a date. Then keep this book with you throughout the day and write down what you do at the times listed below. Then when you're an old person, you can look back and say, "Hey! I remember what I did in the past!" It'll warm your heart.

What is the date today?

8:00 a.m.

10:00 a.m.

12:00 p.m.

2:00 p.m.

4:00 p.m.

6:00 p.m.

8:00 p.m.

Build a BMO

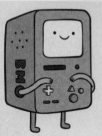

What does it take to be BMO? A LOT OF STUFF, THANK YOU FOR ASKING. But BMO wasn't built in a day. It was made with tender, loving care. What are you made of? Take a look at this list and mark off the best ingredients!

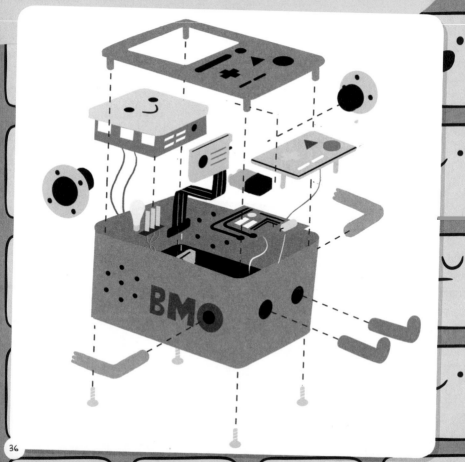

If someone were building you, what would be the three main ingredients?

1. _____

2. _____

3. _____

☐ A heart

☐ Hot-dog water

☐ Sweetness

☐ A third eye

☐ Unlimited tacos

☐ Compliments

☐ Soda pop

☐ Funny jokes

☐ Many smiles

☐ A sense of adventure

☐ Lots and lots of circuits

☐ Comic books

☐ A soul

☐ Ice-cream cakes

☐ Computery stuff

☐ Teddy bears

☐ A rocket launcher

☐ Nice feelings

☐ Stars

☐ Magic beans

☐ The coolest sword EVER

BMO Quiz!

How well do you
know BMO? Take this
quiz and find out!

1. BMO's most prized possession
is its controller. **TRUE** or **FALSE**

2. Finn rescued BMO from the trash.

TRUE or **FALSE**

3. BMO is friends with a bubble. **TRUE** or **FALSE**

4. BMO's tears are triangles. **TRUE** or **FALSE**

5. BMO likes playing soccer. **TRUE** or **FALSE**

6. BMO can make fart noises. **TRUE** or **FALSE**

7. Only Jake can speak to BMO directly.

TRUE or **FALSE**

8. BMO's secret ingredient is clouds.

TRUE or **FALSE**

9. BMO found a baby called Sparkle that it
named Ricky. **TRUE** or **FALSE**

10. BMO drinks gasoline for energy.

TRUE or **FALSE**

What is the name of the song that BMO sings to Finn and Jake after they got in a fight?
A. "Friends"
B. "No More Drama"
C. "Stop the Insanity"
D. "Let's Stay Together"

BMO has which of these things?
A. Charisma!
B. A lot of attitude
C. Secrets
D. A heart of gold

Sometimes BMO pretends it is another person called... ?
A. Randy Butternubs
B. Football
C. NONE OF YOUR BEESWAX, LADY
D. Francine

What is BMO's favorite song?
A. "No Wonder I" by Lake
B. "I Will Be Your Friend" by the Fog
C. "BMO's Rap" by Football & Da Touchdownz
D. "Baby" by the Jiggler

What is the name of the person who created BMO?
A. Princess Bubblegum
B. The Creator
C. Moseph "Moe" Mastro Giovanni
D. Finn

Which of these is NOT one of BMO's playable games?
A. *Kompy's Kastle*
B. *Super Good Boys*
C. *Galaga*
D. *Exciting Hamburger with Cheese*

ARE YOU DONE? I'M BORED.

YOU KNOW A LOT ABOUT ME. LET'S GO PLAY VIDEO GAMES.

ROCK 'N' ROLL
VAMPIRES, UNDEAD BEINGS & WIZARDS

There are a lot of weird and wild things in the Land of Ooo, but don't be frightened. If you have to hold someone's hand, that's totally okay. Check off the things that make you scared.

- ☐ Getting caught in a spiderweb
- ☐ Grandfather hands
- ☐ Losing a tooth
- ☐ Donny
- ☐ A wig made of worms
- ☐ Finding a dollar on the street
- ☐ Getting lost in a supermarket
- ☐ Seeing people cry

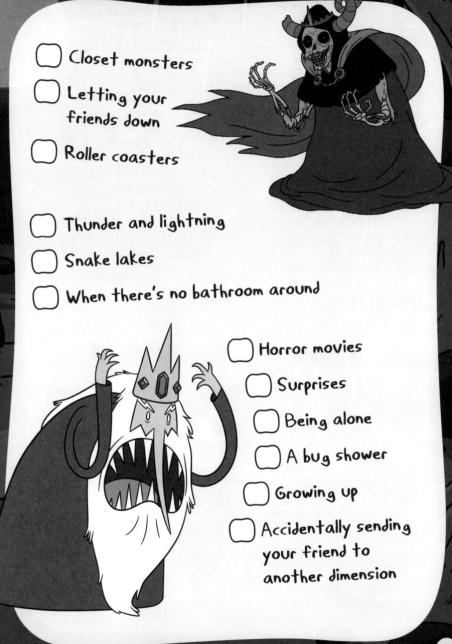

- ☐ Closet monsters
- ☐ Letting your friends down
- ☐ Roller coasters

- ☐ Thunder and lightning
- ☐ Snake lakes
- ☐ When there's no bathroom around

- ☐ Horror movies
- ☐ Surprises
- ☐ Being alone
- ☐ A bug shower
- ☐ Growing up
- ☐ Accidentally sending your friend to another dimension

MARCELINE THE ~~VAMPIRE~~ MUSIC QUEEN

Marceline is a rock 'n' roll vampire who shreds on the guitar like a champ! She loves writing songs when she's not thirsty for that red stuff. YOU should write a song too! Follow these steps and you'll be headed in the right direction. Once you get the hang of it, you'll be writing hits in no time.

STEP #1:

Pick a theme for your song . . .

love   friendship   sadness   happiness

STEP #2:

Pick a subject for your song . . .

sports

breakfast sandwiches

a mysterious gem

your best friend

STEP #3:

Now that you have a theme and a subject, it's time for a title. If you're stumped, just think about it like this—if your theme is sadness and your subject is sports, maybe your song title is "Teardrops on the Basketball Court." See? It's fun to come up with a title.

STEP #4:

Write a song! It might seem difficult, but you'll do fine. Writing from your heart is always good advice. Here's a tip—try to make the last word of the first line rhyme with the last word of the second line. Then keep doing that till you have a song!

GO BANANAS

It can be so boring being a Banana Guard.
That's why they pass the time telling really
bad jokes. Maybe YOU can help them be a little funnier?
Answer the questions below and then see if you know the
punch lines to each of the jokes on the opposite page.
(And check the Answer Key in the back if you need help.)

What do you think is funny?

....

Who is your funniest friend or family member?

....

Write down a joke that you know:

....

....

....

....

....

Why do bananas use sunscreen when they go swimming?

Did you hear the joke about the roof?

What do you call cheese that isn't yours?

What do you call an alligator detective?

WHICH WIZARD ARE YOU?

There are a bunch of wizards running around the Land of Ooo. Some of them are nice, some of them are mean, and some of them are straight-up weirdos. Take this quiz, tally up your answers, and find out which one YOU are!

What do you like to do for fun?

A. Zap people with magic

B. Prance

C. Steal people's memories

D. Teach Finn how to become the Ultimate Wizard

Where is your favorite place to hang out?

A. The forest

B. A rainbow

C. The streets of Wizard City

D. Inside a toad's vocal sack

What's your power?

A. Shooting electric bolts and hovering

B. Turning stuff into butterflies

C. Magic powder

D. Living to be 847 years old

What's your motto?

A. "Now YOU'RE the weenus!"

B. "My body is squishy!"

C. "What's all this hullabaloo?"

D. "Are you ready for more magic?"

What is your favorite thing to wear?

A. A kimono

B. A fanny pack

C. A Mohawk

D. Wizard hats

If you could have dinner with anyone in the universe, who would it be?

A. My Crabbit Familiar

B. A unicorn

C. Marceline

D. Bella Noche

How would you describe yourself?

A. Sadistic

B. Harmless

C. Arrogant

D. A bunch of tadpoles

If you chose mostly option **A**, you are . . . Maja the Sky Witch!

If you chose mostly option **B**, you are . . . Abracadaniel!

If you chose mostly option **C**, you are . . . Ash!

If you chose mostly option **D**, you are . . . the Bufo!

PRINCESS TIME

The Land of Ooo is covered in princesses. They're seriously everywhere! Princess Bubblegum is probably the most famous princess around. She's always cooking up crazy stuff in her laboratory, but she's having a hard time deciding which inventions she likes. Help her out by choosing the ones that sound the coolest!

- ☐ Liquid pizza
- ☐ A formula that brings the dead back to life
- ☐ Robot clones
- ☐ A time machine
- ☐ The perfect sandwich
- ☐ Shoes made of stars
- ☐ A hat that can change other people's minds

- ☐ Chocolate hot tubs
- ☐ Sunglasses that can see your soul
- ☐ A helicopter crown
- ☐ A hug machine
- ☐ A really warm coat that can travel to other dimensions
- ☐ Gloves that shoot tiny lasers
- ☐ A freeze ray
- ☐ The perfect snake-holder
- ☐ A tiny giant
- ☐ A trap that catches rainstorms
- ☐ Cupcake cannons
- ☐ A mustache warmer
- ☐ Kitten mittens

INVENTION CONVENTION

Maybe it's time YOU invented some cool stuff. The first part of this challenge will help you brainstorm some ideas. Choose something from Column A and something from Column B, then SMASH them together to make a new invention. Describe your invention on the label, and remember, this is the Land of Ooo—anything is possible!

COLUMN A:

Cheese

Ice

Laser

Bouncy Ball

Purple

Mystic

Electronic

Candy

Flaming

Lumpy

Vampire

Diamond

Horned

Snowy

Sweet

COLUMN B:

Cannon

Dune Buggy

Monster

Wand

Knapsack

Blaster

Machine

Robot

Skateboard

Camera

Hat

Book

Collar

Crossbow

Mask

What is the name of your invention?

....

What does it do?

....

What does it use for fuel?

....

Where can you buy one?

....

Tell us a story about the first time you used it:

....

....

....

....

....

....

THE ULTIMATE PRINCESS QUIZ

Do you know your princesses? Take this ULTIMATE quiz and find out!

1. Billy once rescued Cotton Candy Princess from the Fire Count. **TRUE or FALSE**

2. Embryo Princess will one day grow to become Baby Princess. **TRUE or FALSE**

3. Emerald Princess is very talkative. **TRUE or FALSE**

4. Ghost Princess was once called Warrior Princess. **TRUE or FALSE**

5. Hot Dog Princess hates Finn. **TRUE or FALSE**

6. Desert Princess got her name because she is made of sand. **TRUE or FALSE**

7. Princess Monster Wife has one of Elbow Princess's hips. **TRUE or FALSE**

8. Orange Princess can only see the color orange. **TRUE or FALSE**

9. Turtle Princess is head of the library in the Land of Ooo. **TRUE or FALSE**

10. Purple Princess uses a computer to communicate. **TRUE or FALSE**

What is the name of Hot Dog Princess's elite guard?

A. The Weiner Brigade

B. Lords of the Frankfurter

C. Hot Dog Knights

D. Sausage Squad

What is Princess Cookie's nickname?

A. Biscuit Betty

B. Baby Snaps

C. Sandra Snickerdoodle

D. Saltine

The Breakfast Kingdom is ruled by which two sisters?

A. Breakfast Princess and Toast Princess

B. Breakfast Princess and Scrambled Egg Princess

C. Sausage Princess and Biscuit Princess

D. The French Toast Sisters

What is the name of Slime Princess's younger sister?

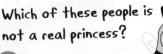

A. Oooza

B. Blargetha

C. Plopina DeGlop

D. Candace

Which of these people is not a real princess?

A. Bee Princess

B. Bounce House Princess

C. Engagement Ring Princess

D. Toilet Princess

Which of these princesses was given a cursed engagement ring by the Ice King?

A. Cursed Engagement Ring Princess

B. Muscle Princess

C. Raggedy Princess

D. Old Lady Princess

THE HOT SEAT

Uh-oh. Flame Princess has got you in the hot seat and there's no escape. Now you're going to have to answer a bunch of questions before she lets you go. The questions are kind of personal but also important to think about. Flame Princess really likes to get to know people, huh?

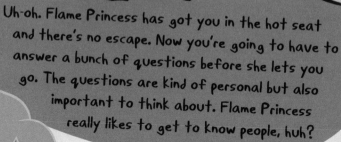

What makes you happy?

....

....

What makes you sad?

....

....

What's a nice thing you've done for someone else?

....

....

What's a thing you've done that you wish you didn't do?

....

....

Who is someone you look up to?

....

Who is someone you don't know but would like to know?

....

If you could eat dinner with anyone in the Land of Ooo, who would it be, and why?

....

....

....

If you could go anywhere in the universe, where would you go, and why?

....

....

....

WHAT'S THAT PRINCESS THINKIN'?

Princess Princess Princess is really emotional right now. You might be, too, if you had a whole bunch of princess heads. Each part of Princess Princess Princess has her own thoughts and opinions, that's for sure. What are her heads thinking? Only YOU know for certain. Answer this question and then sort it out.

If you could be made up of five different people, who would they be, and why?

....

....

....

....

....

....

FINNCESS TIME

Princess Bubblegum used her Princess-Making Machine on Finn, and now he's been turned into a **Finncess**. Everyone is freaking out. No one knows what's going to happen next. There are so many unanswered questions. What would YOU do in a situation like this?

What's your princess name?

....

What would your first royal announcement be?

....

Who would be the leader of your royal guard?

....

What would you protect yourself with?

....

What would your kingdom be called?

....

Turn Finn into the mightiest princess that the Land of Ooo has ever seen. Make sure you list all of the ingredients to make an awesome royal rump-kicker.

INGREDIENTS:

....

....

....

CANDY KINGDOM

Welcome to the Candy Kingdom, where the air is sweet and the people are sweeter. Get to know some of them a little bit better by taking this quiz!

1. Ice Cream Guy is married to Toffee Princess. **TRUE** or **FALSE**

2. Dr. Dextrose has given a speech on the future of cuteness. **TRUE** or **FALSE**

3. Someone took a bite out of Grape Popsicle Guy. **TRUE** or **FALSE**

4. Ice Cream Lady is actually made of whipped cream. **TRUE** or **FALSE**

5. Dr. Donut does not have a scientific parasite. **TRUE** or **FALSE**

6. Candy Magician has always been the best magician in the Land of Ooo. **TRUE** or **FALSE**

Who is this?

A. Donut No-Hole

B. Pecan Sandy

C. Cinnamon Bun

D. Pastry Peter

60

What is Taffy Girl made of?

A. Vanilla

B. Taffy

C. Creamsicle

D. I don't know, but she looks weird.

Which of these characters is a talking piñata?

A. Manfried

B. Speaky, the Talking Piñata

C. Chatterbox

D. Carmela, the Talking Piñata

Who is Cherry Cream Soda married to?

A. Root Beer Float

B. Soda Jerk

C. Root Beer Guy

D. Steven

Which of these groups loves to get in fights?

A. The Punch Club

B. The Marshmallow Kids

C. The Froot Frat

D. The Cotton Candy Circus

Who put Princess Bubblegum in a milk suit when she turned green and lost her hair?

A. Dr. Pudding

B. Nurse Pound Cake

C. Pie Guy, the Private Eye

D. Dr. Ice Cream

Which character lives in the Candy Kingdom but is technically not candy?

A. Taco Tina

B. Punch Bowl

C. Glenn

D. Martin

Who is the Candy Kingdom's resident grave digger?

A. Candy Corn Grandma

B. Starchy

C. Dark Chocolate Drizzle

D. The Frosting Giant

PEPPERMINT BUTLER'S
GUIDE TO
MANNERS

Peppermint Butler is a fancy-pants who is very particular when it comes to manners. He's got all sorts of rules about how to be. Answer this quick quiz and then figure out which things in the list on the opposite page are either a DO or a DON'T.

What are three of your bad habits?

1._____   2._____   3._____

What are three of your good habits?

1._____   2._____   3._____

What is a bad habit you have that you would like to change?

....

....

What is a good habit that you wish more people had?

....

....

DO		DON'T
☐	Burping at the dinner table	☑
☑	Saying "please" and "thank you"	☐
☐	Picking your toenails	☑
☑	Falling asleep during math class	☐
☑	Holding a door open for someone	☐
☑	Farting	☐
☐	Tickling your little sister till she wets her pants	☑
☑	Helping an elderly person across the street	☐
☑	Smiling	☐
☐	Eating your boogers	☑
☐	Littering	☑
☑	Saying "I love you" to people that you love	☐
☑	Eating all your dinner	☐
☐	Cleaning your room	☐
☐	Leaving a surprise in the toilet	☑
☑	Being nice to people	☐
☑	Picking up trash when you see it on the ground	☐
☑	Brushing and flossing your teeth	☐
☑	Saving money	☐

SWEET FACES

How well do you know the Candy People?
See if you can identify the pictured characters
using the word bank below. Tell a funny fact about
each one of them, too, while you're at it.

Smudge

Cookie Guy

Starchy

Crunchy

Cinnamon Bun   Manfried   Goliad

Gingerbread Chap   Dr. Dextrose

Pinky Piez   Cinnamon Buddy   Dr. J

Peppermint Butler   Creama

THE CANDY KINGDOM
AWARDS

It's time for the Candy Kingdom Awards, when the best and brightest come out to be honored. This time around, YOU get to choose who wins. You can choose options from the word bank or make up your own. It's fun to win stuff. Sweet victory!

Name three of your talents.

1. .... 2. .... 3. ....

What award would you like to win?

....

- Sweetest
- Best Dressed
- Most Likely to Get Eaten
- Sugar Daddy
- Sour Puss
- Biggest Sucker
- Best Sprinkles
- Jelliest
- Most Sour
- Most Likely to Give You a Toothache

Mr. Cupcakes

Stormo

Crunchy

Donut Guy

Gelatin Man

Jam Jam

Tart Toter

Peppermint Butler

Chocoberry

CANDY CUTOUT

Wouldn't it be cool to have some Candy People paper action figures? Use safety scissors to cut out the figures on the opposite page. Then cut out some of the word balloons on the following page and make the Candy People have a conversation. You can pretend they're at a cool party, or maybe they're talking about how the Earl of Lemongrab is weird.

HAVE FUN!

SOUR PATCH

The Earl of Lemongrab overheard you talking about him, and he is not happy. NOT HAPPY! He has a lot of weird rules, too. Do YOU have any rules? They don't have to be weird, but if they are, that's okay.

What are three rules that you follow?

1. .... 2. .... 3. ....

What are three rules that people don't follow as much as they should?

1. .... 2. .... 3. ....

What are three new rules that you think everyone should follow?

1. .... 2. .... 3. ....

Which of these rules would you follow?

- ☐ Pants must always be worn in the swimming pool
- ☐ No wearing hats indoors
- ☐ You must read at least one book a month
- ☐ Potato chips must be eaten with milk and only on Tuesdays
- ☑ Be kind to people even if they're not very nice
- ☐ Magic wands cannot be used to turn people into kitties
- ☐ No rocking out after 6:00 p.m.
- ☑ If you need help, don't be afraid to ask for it
- ☐ Do not squeeze the lemons
- ☐ Compliment somebody every day
- ☐ HUGGING IS FORBIDDEN

WOULD YOU RATHER?

Spending time with the Earl of Lemongrab isn't that fun. What would YOU rather do? Circle your answers and then make a wish for fun.

Get your hair braided **OR** Get your tooth pulled

Watch a movie **OR** Watch a football game

Play on the computer **OR** Live your life to the fullest

Laugh **OR** Cry

Talk on the telephone **OR** Look for ancient relics

Tickle **OR** Tackle

Skateboard through a park **OR** Fly high atop the clouds

Be a cyclops **OR** Be a unicorn

Tap dance **OR** Belly dance

Play tennis **OR** Play a board game

Wear your hair in a Mohawk **OR** Shave your head

Talk to your teacher **OR** Talk to your principal

74

Read a book **OR** Play with toys

Drink a dirt milk shake **OR** Eat a pie made of rocks

Learn a new thing every day **OR**
Forget a bad thing every day

Give someone a compliment **OR** Give someone a kiss

Be trapped in a stinky dungeon **OR**
Be trapped in a sweet-smelling dungeon

Win a bunch of money for yourself **OR** Give a bunch of money to someone who really needs it

Wear crazy pajamas on your first day of school
OR Wear your heart on your sleeve

Fight an evil wizard **OR** Fight a vampire

Be a fish **OR** Be a cheetah

Wear shoes that make you fly **OR**
Wear flies who like cool shoes

Play the guitar **OR** Have the guitar play you

Cure a really bad disease **OR**
Discover you're the world's best tap dancer

Ride in a hot-air balloon **OR** Ride a motorcycle

TIMELESS TALES

There are so many stories in the Earldom of Lemongrab, but the Earl of Lemongrab keeps taking out all the words that he doesn't like. It's very rude. YOU should replace them. Use the guide below to help you figure out what kind of word to write in the space.

ADJECTIVE:

NOUN:

ANIMAL (PLURAL):

NOUN:

ADJECTIVE:

ADJECTIVE:

PLACE:

NOUN:

VERB:

PLURAL NOUN:

VERB:

ADJECTIVE:

FAMOUS PHRASE OR SAYING:

Spring had sprung in the Earldom of Lemongrab and the Lemon People were feeling .... The .... was shining and people were taking their .... out for very long walks. But things were far from perfect. The Earl of Lemongrab saw a/an .... pop out of the ground and he didn't like it one bit. He could be a little .... sometimes. So he gathered all of his .... subjects in the middle of (the) .... and told them some bad news.

"If I see one more .... on the street, I will .... you in the dungeon with the ....," he shouted. He really liked to shout.

"Then I will .... all of the people who do not follow my .... rules!" The people began to cry, but the Earl of Lemongrab simply stuck out his tongue and said, "...........................!"

LEMON QUIZ

You think you know the Earl of Lemongrab's world, but you might not. Take this quiz and find out!

1. The Earl of Lemongrab has a clone named Steven. **TRUE or FALSE**

2. The original Earl of Lemongrab is a mean tyrant. **TRUE or FALSE**

3. The Earl of Lemongrab rules over the Earldom of Lemongrab. **TRUE or FALSE**

4. Plop-Top is really good at conversation. **TRUE or FALSE**

5. Lemonjon is a giant who keeps his body parts in separate rooms. **TRUE or FALSE**

What is this?

A. Blarf

B. Lemon Mess

C. Seed-Wad

D. Disgusting

Plop-Top has also gone by which of these names?

A. Dump-Dome

B. Lemon Dropping

C. Lemon Pile

D. Cynthia

Where does the Earl of Lemongrab live?

A. In a condo by the beach

B. Castle Lemongrab

C. Lemongrab Acres

D. Sourtown

Lemongrab 2 was created by which of these people?

A. Princess Lemonade

B. The Earl of Lemongrab

C. Princess Bubblegum

D. Dr. Squeezington

Finn once sat next to a Lemon Person with which of these names?

A. Duke Suck-Lemon

B. Admiral Sourpuss

C. Lemonjon

D. Limey

What is Lemonhope's full name?

A. Terry Lemonhope Jr.

B. Badlemonnohope

C. The Earl of Lemonhope

D. CLASSIFIED

How many times has the Earl of Lemongrab been mentioned in this quiz?

A. 6

B. 7

C. 8

D. Who cares?

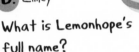

CHILLIN' WITH THE ICE KING

The Ice Kingdom is the domain of the mighty ICE KING. Beware his frosty wrath! Okay, who are we kidding? His wrath is only kind of chilly. Here's the deal—Ice King can get pretty lonely, and it makes him a cranky pants. What makes you a cranky pants? Take this quiz and see!

What are three things that annoy you?

1. .... 2. .... 3. ....

What are three things that excite you?

1. .... 2. .... 3. ....

Where do you go to be alone?

....

....

....

....

....

....

Which of these things are totally NOT COOL?

Loud music **COOL** or **NOT COOL**

Falling asleep with your eyes open **COOL** or **NOT COOL**

Calling someone rude names **COOL** or **NOT COOL**

Kidnapping princesses **COOL** or **NOT COOL**

Being a bro **COOL** or **NOT COOL**

Cleaning up penguin droppings **COOL** or **NOT COOL**

Knowing all about ancient artifacts **COOL** or **NOT COOL**

Not listening **COOL** or **NOT COOL**

Making a birthday cake **COOL** or **NOT COOL**

People who are all up in my business **COOL** or **NOT COOL**

Gossiping **COOL** or **NOT COOL**

Hair extensions **COOL** or **NOT COOL**

Friendship **COOL** or **NOT COOL**

The Imagination Zone **COOL** or **NOT COOL**

Wicked drum solos **COOL** or **NOT COOL**

Pushing over trash cans **COOL** or **NOT COOL**

The Demonic Wishing Eye **COOL** or **NOT COOL**

Drawing a mustache on your school photo **COOL** or **NOT COOL**

High fives **COOL** or **NOT COOL**

Screaming for no reason **COOL** or **NOT COOL**

GUNTER!

Gunter is Ice King's #1 fan. Or is that Gunther? Maybe it's Gunthy? Let's get real for a minute—all of Ice King's Gunters look exactly alike. It feels really good to finally say that. It's time for some of them to stand out. Give these guys some personality!

What do you do to stand out?

Whom do people tell you that you look like?

How does it make you feel?

What would you do if you had a twin?

NAME:

OCCUPATION:

MOTTO:

FAVORITE FOOD:

NAME:

OCCUPATION:

MOTTO:

FAVORITE SPORT:

NAME:

OCCUPATION:

MOTTO:

FAVORITE MOVIE:

HELPFUL HINT: A motto is a saying that captures a person's outlook on life, like "Always be like a piano—upright and grand!" or "Nice guys finish first!"

ICE
QUIZ

How well do you know Ice King? Take this quiz and find out. Don't freeze up!

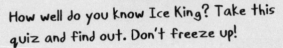

1. Gunter has his own keyboard. **TRUE** or **FALSE**

2. Ice King has a tattoo on his butt. **TRUE** or **FALSE**

3. The Ice Kingdom is actually made of salt. **TRUE** or **FALSE**

4. Finn is Ice King's biological son. **TRUE** or **FALSE**

5. Ice King once disguised himself as Finn. **TRUE** or **FALSE**

6. Ice King's beard sometimes has a mind of its own. **TRUE** or **FALSE**

What is the name of the song that Ice King sings after trapping Finn in the Spirit World?

A. "Finn Is FIN"

B. "Trapped in the Spirit World"

C. "Ice King's Song of Joy"

D. "Wannabe"

Which of these powers does Ice King possess?

A. The ability to make a pretty good flan

B. Future Vision

C. Wizard Eyes

D. The Power of Positive Thinking

Which of these things has Ice King used as a disguise?

A. Princess Monster Wife

B. A poo-brained horse

C. The Cloak of Secrets

D. Gunter

Which of these things has Ice King NOT said?

A. "How about a smooch pooch, my little candy gram?"

B. "Your hat is stupid!"

C. "This is my domain!"

D. "Gunter was preggers!"

What is Ice King's real name?

A. Simon Frost

B. Simon Petrikov

C. Chill Baby

D. Destiny Freeze

Who owns this drum kit?

A. Ice King

B. Gunter

C. Rebecca Sugar

D. Drum Warehouse

Which name did Ice King give the Banana Guard when he tried to stop Princess Bubblegum's potluck?

A. Butterface

B. Mr. Garamblington

C. Nice King

D. He didn't give them a name

What is the key to Ice King's power?

A. His robe

B. His mood

C. His key

D. His crown

FIONNA & CAKE

All of Ice King's fan fic has been erased!
His stories about Fionna and Cake are gone!
In case you didn't know, FAN FIC is short for "fan
fiction," which is just another name for stories written by
a fan. Now it's time for YOU to write some fan fic about
Fionna and Cake. Don't listen to the haters—get creative!

GRAYBLES 'N' THINGS

A Grayble is just like a short story, and this one has been left unfinished! Use your imagination and create a Grayble of your own. Make sure it has a beginning, a middle, and an end. It can be about anything you want. Maybe Finn gets trapped in the belly of a living ball of hair? Maybe YOU fall through a portal and end up as the Ice King's prisoner? The possibilities are endless. GO NUTS!

It was a bright and sunny day in the Land of Ooo UNTIL . . .

LINGO BINGO

Finn and Jake are very hip. Did you know they own A SCARF? It's true. They also use a lot of hip words like "shmowzow" and "dude." Who knows what any of it means? Make up a bunch of NEW hip words for them to use and make sure they shout them out.

DUDE!

SLAMACOW!

RHOMBUS!

WRONGTEOUS!

MOMMY!

COOL!
MATHEMATICAL!
ALGEBRAIC!
AWESOME!
RIGHTEOUS!
RADICAL!
SHMOWZOW!

TREE TRUNKS & MR. PIG GO ON AN ADVENTURE

Tree Trunks and Mr. Pig are on a romantic date, but they need YOU to help them out. Ask your friends for the parts of speech listed below, then transfer their answers to the story.

ADJECTIVE:
....

ANIMAL:
....

ADJECTIVE:
....

PLURAL NOUN:
....

PLACE:
....

NOUN:
....

PLACE:
....

ADJECTIVE:
....

TYPE OF FOOD:
....

NOUN:
....
....

In was a bright .... day in the Land of Ooo when

Tree Trunks spotted a/an .... in the sky. It reminded

her of how much she loved her .... boyfriend, Mr. Pig.

She put down her basket filled with sweet .... ,

tied a bow on her tail, and took off to meet Mr. Pig at (the)

.... When Tree Trunks got there, Mr. Pig gave

her a/an .... and kissed her on the cheek.

"Let's go on an adventure, my dear Tree Trunks," said Mr. Pig.

"We can go to the magical land of .... and

explore the .... caverns. Then we can eat some

.... and cuddle under the starlight." Tree Trunks

smiled, and off they went! But something was weighing heavy

on Tree Trunks's mind that stopped them dead in their tracks.

"Oh no! I left my .... in the oven," said Tree Trunks.

Mr. Pig grinned from ear to ear. "You mean this?" asked Mr.

Pig. He remembered to check the oven before they left, and Tree

Trunks was thankful. The couple gave each other a kiss on the

cheek and continued on to their next adventure.

FAMILY TIME

There's nothing more important than family.
Sometimes your friends can be your family
and your family can be your friends. Isn't that cool?
In the Land of Ooo, there are all kinds of different
families. What would YOU do for yours?

What are three qualities that a good family should have?

1. .... 2. .... 3. ....

Who is a friend that you're so close to, it's almost like
they're family?

....

Who is a family member that has always been there for you?

....

Who is a family member that
you've always been there for?

....

....

....

I WOULD . . .

- ☑ Pick my uncle up at the airport
- ☑ Help my mom fight a wizard
- ☑ Show my cousin how to fish
- ☐ Perform a magic act for my family
- ☐ Cheer up my dad if he was having a bad day
- ☑ Make cookies with my mom
- ☑ Help my best friend fight a dragon
- ☐ Trick my brother into eating goo
- ☐ Hide my sister's favorite book
- ☑ Scare the heebie-jeebies out of my cousin

- ☐ Let me aunt kiss me on the cheek as much as she wants
- ☐ Turn my uncle into a cyborg
- ☑ Always be there for my family when they need me
- ☐ Trap my brother in a cage
- ☐ Invite my best friend to a family dinner
- ☑ Help my mom paint a flowerpot
- ☑ Turn my dad into a dark avenger of the night
- ☐ Dress up my brother in old lady clothes
- ☐ Chase my sister around the yard
- ☑ Love my friends and family no matter what

LADY RAINICORN
& THE PUPS

Jake and Lady Rainicorn have got a lot of love, a lot of pups, and NO TIME. Things can get pretty hectic, so when the whole family gets together, they like to play games. What kinds of games do you play with your family? OH OH OH! You should totally make up some NEW games using the titles below. Or just create your own. Either way—FUN!

What are your top three favorite games?

1. _____ 2. _____ 3. _____

Which family member do you have the most fun with?

....

Have you ever cheated? If so, how did it make you feel?

....

....

....

PS: CHEATING ISN'T COOL.

CrazyQuest Vampire Trivia

EXTREME Patty-Cake Wiener Winner

Lumpy Space Race

Super Card Shark

Hide & Go Nap Where's My Thing?

GAME TITLE: ....

CREATOR: ....

HOW TO PLAY: ....

....

....

....

GAME TITLE: ....

CREATOR: ....

HOW TO PLAY: ....

....

....

....

FAMILY QUIZ TIME

There are a lot of families in the Land of Ooo. Take this quiz and see how well you know them.

1. Finn was adopted by Jake's parents, Joshua and Margaret.

   TRUE or **FALSE**

2. Lumpy Space King refers to Lumpy Space Princess as "daughter."

   TRUE or **FALSE**

3. Finn has a baby sister in Farmworld.

   TRUE or **FALSE**

4. When Lumpy Space People get married, they become one person.

   TRUE or **FALSE**

5. When Finn's parents found him, he was soiled and stuck to a leaf.

   TRUE or **FALSE**

6. Flame Princess has fourteen younger brothers.

   TRUE or **FALSE**

Which statement best describes this family?

A. These people are polar bears.

B. These people love french fries.

C. These people are crazy.

D. These people are nuts.

Who is this?

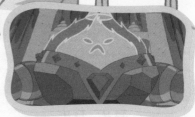

A. Flame King

B. Flame Princess's older brother

C. Dirk Blazington, Fire King

D. Cameron, Flame Princess's cousin

Who wrote the book Mind Games?

A. Clarence

B. Kevin

C. Jay T. Doggzone

D. Joke the Hog

What is this?

A. The music box that Margaret used to soothe Jake and Finn

B. The shape that Jake becomes when he misses his mom

C. A nutcracker Finn made for his dad

D. Priceless

Can you name each of Lady Rainicorn's pups?

Use the options bank to help you.

1

2

3

4

5

T.V.   Charlie

Kim Kil Whan

Viola   Jake Jr.

Which of these is not a title used by the Nuts Royal Family?

A. Marquis

B. El Capitan

C. Duke

D. Duchess

FRIENDS OF OOO

There are so many awesome dudes in the Land of Ooo, it's actually hard to keep track of them all. Take this quiz and see how many you know!

1. Trami and Tromo are members of the Destiny Gang. **TRUE** or **FALSE**

2. Members of the Hyooman tribe wear weird animal-themed hats. **TRUE** or **FALSE**

3. Bucket Knight can grow in size if you pour water on him. **TRUE** or **FALSE**

4. Forest Cyclops's tears can heal any injury. **TRUE** or **FALSE**

5. Crab Demon is covered in all-seeing eyes. **TRUE** or **FALSE**

The Flying Lettuce Brothers are which of these things?

A. Brothers

B. Lettuce

C. Criminals

D. ALL OF THE ABOVE

Who is this?

A. Lisby the Cashew Butler

B. Peanut Pascal

C. Limbs Nutterberg

D. Legume Larry

Who is the leader of the Destiny Gang?

A. Amanda Destiny

B. Big Destiny

C. Destiny Schwartz

D. Chance

Who owns Pudding's Hardware?

A. Your mom

B. Finn & Jake

C. The Pudding Company

D. Buck Pudding

Who is this?

A. Itchy, the Medi-Clownette

B. Barry!

C. Head Clown Nurse

D. Doctor Giggles

Where do Lub Glubs live?

A. Inside our minds

B. Inside inflatable pool toys

C. Right off of I-75

D. Glubville

Who is this?

A. Fionna

B. Lady Finn

C. Big Barbara

D. Susan Strong

MYSTERY DUNGEON

What would you do if you woke up in a Mystery Dungeon? This is a big deal, so answer these questions carefully. Then write a story about what might happen if you and your friends found yourself trapped in a Mystery Dungeon. Would it be fun? Would it be bad? It can be anything you want.

If you had to be trapped in a Mystery Dungeon, who are three people that you would want to be trapped with?

1. .... 2. .... 3. ....

Have you ever been trapped somewhere? If so, where?

....

....

What item would you bring with you to a deserted island?

....

....

....

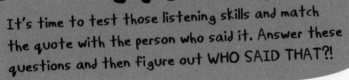

WHO SAID THAT?!

It's time to test those listening skills and match the quote with the person who said it. Answer these questions and then figure out WHO SAID THAT?!

What is a catchphrase that you use a lot?

....

....

What is a slang word that you use with your friends?

....

What is a word that you've completely made up?

....

What does it mean?

....

....

....

"Battery low. Shutdown imminent."

"People make mistakes. It's part of growing up, and you never stop growing."

"I eat shades of red."

"It's gonna be so flippin' awesome!"

"Dude, be calmed by my saliva!"

"Even if we like each other, we're still going to hurt each other!"

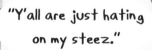
"Y'all are just hating on my steez."

"Imagination is for turbo-nerds who can't handle how kick-butt reality is!"

WHO ARE THESE PEOPLE?

Can you identify all of these people? I sure hope so. Tell a funny fact about each one of them, too, while you're at it.

....

....

....

....

....

....

....

....

WOULD YOU RATHER?

The Land of Ooo is filled with difficult decisions.
Which would YOU rather do?

Kiss an angry octopus **OR** High-five a tiger

Do the hula **OR** Do the twist

Be a Lumpy Space Person **OR** Be a Candy Person

Eat a bowl of hair **OR** Stick your foot in a bucket of scorpions

Play your music loud **OR** Go to jail

Put your hand on a hot stove **OR** Listen to the Earl of Lemongrab

Roughhouse with a Marauder **OR** Go on a date with Gary the Mermaid Queen

Drink a bottle of goo **OR** Eat a goo burger

Be warm **OR** Be cold

Hug a cactus **OR** Get a shot in the arm

Have a face on your butt like Cute King **OR** Live on GOLB's tongue

Be a hat **OR** Be underwear

Play a lyre **OR** Have two giant horns

Be Lumpy Space Princess's boyfriend **OR** Be Lumpy Space Princess's enemy

Kiss the Ice King **OR** Hug the Flame King

Wear a key tied around your head **OR** Be a Business Man

Be a butterfly with a laser gun **OR** Be a Forest Cyclops

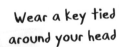

LUMPS IN SPACE

Welcome to Lumpy Space, home of the lumpiest space princess in the Land of Ooo! (You know that's Lumpy Space Princess, right? Just checking.) But do you know everything there is to know about Lumpy Space? Take this quiz and see!

1. Lumpy Space looks like a giant waterslide.   **TRUE** or **FALSE**

2. If the Lumpy Space Reactor Core explodes, it means big trouble.   **TRUE** or **FALSE**

3. Lumpy Space People do not trust "non-lumpers."   **TRUE** or **FALSE**

4. Lumpy Space Princess's parents don't like her saying "lump."   **TRUE** or **FALSE**

5. Everyone in Lumpy Space can wish themselves into having legs and feet.   **TRUE** or **FALSE**

6. Lumpy Space Princess hates to be the center of attention.   **TRUE** or **FALSE**

7. Lumpy Space Princess considers Finn a real friend.   **TRUE** or **FALSE**

What happens if Lumpy Space Princess bites you?

A. You bleed

B. You become lumpy

C. No one knows!

D. Absolutely nothing

Where is the portal that takes you to Lumpy Space?

A. Inside our imagination!

B. Over by that one weird tree that everyone thinks is watching them

C. Inside Finn's knapsack

D. Inside the Cotton Candy Forest, in the mouth of a frog who is sitting on a mushroom

What is the password to the portal to Lumpy Space?

A. LUMPS4LIFE

B. Whatevers2009

C. Password1234

D. Please

What is the name of the weekly dance that happens in Lumpy Space?

A. One Enchanted Evening

B. Lumps Under the Stars

C. Promcoming

D. Macarena Monday

What do Lumpy Space People call "non-lumpers" who are not lumpy?

A. Smoothies

B. BOGUS

C. Anything they want

D. People

Who is LSP's ex-boyfriend?

A. Finn

B. Brad

C. BMO

D. Jake

LUMPY SPACE
JOURNAL

LSP lives such an exciting life. She's always going to very fancy royal events where she's the center of attention. Brad is so jealous of her extravagant lifestyle. Can you imagine what her journal must look like? Check out the Lumpy Space People below and write an entry from LSP's secret diary using some of them. Make sure it's super melodramatic.

LENNY

GLASSES

MELISSA

BRAD

MONTY

LUMPY SPACE
MASK

The hottest costume once again this season is Lumpy Space Princess! You don't even have to be invited to a costume party to wear the super-hot LSP mask. You'll be the talk of the village (or wherever you live) in this little number. Wear it for fun or to scare someone into marrying you! (And answer these questions, too, while you're at it.)

What is your favorite costume?

....

....

What style clothes do you like to wear?

....

What's your favorite color?

....

What's a funny piece of clothing that you own?

....

....

INTO THE
FUTURE

The dynamic duo is back, and the future is bright! Do you ever wish you could see yourself years from now? Maybe you'll be the President of the Universe one day. Who knows? Answer these questions and use the Future Crystal to predict YOUR FUTURE.

What will you be doing in five years?

What will you be doing in ten years?

....

....

....

....

....

What will you be doing in fifteen years?

....

....

....

....

What will you be doing in twenty years?

....

....

....

....

....

SUPER-SECRET SPY STUFF

Jake and Finn are using a secret language to make plans for the weekend. Are they going to build a rocket and travel into space? Maybe they just want to build a pizza oven? Answer these questions and then you can put words in their mouths. But no one can know, so hush up about it.

Do you and your friends have a secret language?

....

What words have you made up together?

....

....

What games have you created with your friends?

....

....

Do you and your friends have a special place where you hang out?

....

....

THE LAND OF
DREAMS

Finn had a crazy dream, but he kind of forgot it.
You know how that happens with dreams sometimes?
Sometimes you need a little help filling in the blanks.
Answer these questions and then use the other page
as a dream journal. What do YOU dream about?

- [ ] Flying
- [ ] Cheeseburgers
- [ ] Parties
- [x] Not wearing any clothes
- [x] Fighting a serpent king
- [ ] Dancing

- [ ] A mountain that comes alive and eats you
- [ ] Sleeping
- [ ] More dreams
- [ ] One day doing your taxes

DATE:
....

WHAT HAPPENED IN MY DREAM:
....

....

....

....

....

....

DATE:
....

WHAT HAPPENED IN MY DREAM:
....

....

....

....

....

....

ARE YOU A FINN, A JAKE, OR A YOU?

Here it is. Are you ready? This quiz will tell you if you're more like Jake the Dog or Finn the Human. Can you stand it? Quick—TAKE THIS TEST!

What is your favorite food?

A. Ice cream

B. Meat loaf

What's your favorite color?

A. I'm colorblind

B. Baby blue

What is an interesting thing about you?

A. I wear transparent pants made by pixies

B. In a past life, I was named Shoko

Who would you take on a wild adventure?

A. My best friend

B. My best friend

What is your weapon of choice?

A. My body

B. My sword
My mind

Which would you prefer to have?

A. Stretchy arms

B. Beautiful blond hair that you hide under a hat

Who do you have a crush on?

A. Lady Rainicorn

B. Princess Bubblegum

What are you afraid of?

A. Spiders

B. The ocean

What have you been turned into before?

A. A demon

B. A cat

What do you do if you're locked out of your house?

A. Make your finger into a key

B. Build a totally new house that's more awesome than the first one

Turn the page to find out
WHO YOU ARE . . .

125

YOU'RE YOU!

THAT'S THE ANSWER.

It doesn't matter if you're in the Land of Ooo or at your aunt Gertrude's apartment— you're the same you, no matter what. And you're pretty awesome, so don't forget that.

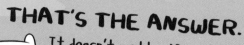

But just in case you wanted to know—if you answered **A** for most of the questions, you're **JAKE**; if you answered **B** for most of the questions, you're **FINN**.

Either way, you're A WINNER.

ANSWER KEY

Jake the Dog: The Quiz (pp. 26-27)

1. TRUE, **2.** TRUE, **3.** FALSE, **4.** TRUE,
5. FALSE, **6.** FALSE, **7.** TRUE, **8.** FALSE,
9. TRUE, **10.** TRUE

C. Begs the Question, **C.** Stretchy Power,
A. The Fruit Witches, **A.** Card Wars,
B. Lady Rainicorn,
D. The energy of a thousand partying demons

Finn the Human: The Quiz (pp. 28-29)

1. TRUE, **2.** TRUE, **3.** FALSE, **4.** TRUE,
5. TRUE, **6.** FALSE, **7.** TRUE, **8.** FALSE,
9. FALSE, **10.** TRUE

D. Meat loaf, **B.** Davey,
D. NONE OF THE ABOVE,
B. A realm full of pillows, **A.** Prince Hotbod,
B. A cat with a box on its head

BMO Quiz! (pp. 38-39)

1. TRUE, **2.** FALSE, **3.** TRUE, **4.** TRUE,
5. TRUE, **6.** TRUE, **7.** FALSE, **8.** FALSE,
9. TRUE, **10.** FALSE

A. "Friends," **D.** A heart of gold, **B.** Football,
A. "No Wonder I" by Lake,
C. Moseph "Moe" Mastro Giovanni,
D. Exciting Hamburger with Cheese

Go Bananas (pp. 44-45)

ANSWER: **So they don't peel!**

ANSWER: **Never mind, it's over your head!**

ANSWER: **Nacho cheese!**

ANSWER: **An investigator!**

The Ultimate Princess Quiz (pp. 52-53)

1. TRUE, **2.** FALSE, **3.** FALSE, **4.** TRUE,
5. FALSE, **6.** TRUE, **7.** TRUE, **8.** TRUE,
9. TRUE, **10.** TRUE

C. Hot Dog Knights, **B.** Baby Snaps,
A. Breakfast Princess and Toast Princess,
B. Blargetha, **D.** Toilet Princess,
D. Old Lady Princess

Candy Kingdom (pp. 60-61)

1. FALSE, **2.** TRUE, **3.** TRUE, **4.** FALSE,
5. TRUE, **6.** FALSE

C. Cinnamon Bun, **B.** Taffy, **A.** Manfried,
C. Root Beer Guy, **B.** The Marshmallow Kids,
D. Dr. Ice Cream, **B.** Punch Bowl, **B.** Starchy

Sweet Faces (pp. 64-65)

IMAGE #1 — **Manfried**

IMAGE #2 — **Starchy**

IMAGE #3 — **Dr. Dextrose**

IMAGE #4 — **Goliad**

Lemon Quiz (pp. 78-79)

1. FALSE, **2.** TRUE, **3.** TRUE, **4.** FALSE,
5. TRUE

C. Seed-Wad, **A.** Dump-Dome, **B.** Castle Lemongrab,
C. Princess Bubblegum, **A.** Duke Suck-Lemon,
B. Badlemonnohope, **B.** 7

Ice Quiz (pp. 84-85)

1. TRUE, **2.** TRUE, **3.** FALSE, **4.** FALSE,
5. TRUE, **6.** TRUE

C. "Ice King's Song of Joy," **C.** Wizard Eyes,
B. A poo-brained horse,
A. "How about a smooch pooch, my little candy gram?",
B. Simon Petrikov, **A.** Ice King,
B. Mr. Garamblington, **D.** His crown

Family Quiz Time (pp. 98-99)

1. TRUE, **2.** TRUE, **3.** FALSE, **4.** TRUE,
5. TRUE, **6.** FALSE

D. These people are nuts, **A.** Flame King,
C. Jay T. Doggzone, **A.** The music box that
Margaret used to soothe Jake and Finn
#1—T.V., **#2**—Viola, **#3**—Jake Jr.,
#4—Charlie, **#5**—Kim Kil Whan, **B.** El Capitan

Friends of Ooo (pp. 100-101)

1. TRUE, **2.** TRUE, **3.** TRUE, **4.** TRUE,
5. FALSE

D. ALL OF THE ABOVE, **A.** Lisby the Cashew
Butler, **B.** Big Destiny, **D.** Buck Pudding,
C. Head Clown Nurse, **B.** Inside inflatable pool toys,
D. Susan Strong

Who Said That?! (pp. 104-105)

"People make mistakes. It's part of growing up, and you
never stop growing." — **Duke of Nuts**

"It's gonna be so flippin' awesome!" — **Lumpy
Space Princess**

"Battery low. Shutdown." — **BMO**

"I eat shades of red." — **Marceline**

"Dude, be calmed by my saliva!" — **Jake**

"Even if we like each other, we're still going
to hurt each other!" — **Flame Princess**

"Imagination is for turbo-nerds who can't handle how
kick-butt reality is!" — **Finn**

"Y'all are just hating on my steez." — **Ice King**

Who Are These People? (pp. 106-107)

IMAGE #1 — **Tree Trunks**

IMAGE #2 — **James Baxter**

IMAGE #3 — **Rattleballs**

IMAGE #4 — **Donny**

IMAGE #5 — **Cosmic Owl**

IMAGE #6 — **Prismo**

Lumps in Space (pp. 110-111)

1. FALSE, **2.** TRUE, **3.** TRUE, **4.** TRUE,
5. FALSE, **6.** FALSE, **7.** TRUE

B. You become lumpy, **D.** Inside the Cotton Candy
Forest, in the mouth of a frog who is sitting on a
mushroom, **B.** Whatevers2009, **C.** Promcoming,
A. Smoothies, **B.** Brad